BOOK OF DREAMS

AF632804

Rahil Najafabadi

BookLeaf Publishing

Presentation by *BookLeaf Publishing*

Web: www.bookleafpub.com

E-mail: info@bookleafpub.com

ISBN: 9789357213097

First edition 2023

There are things that must be said, words that must be written, and pictures that must be painted. Together, apart; it all makes sense with you.

To E

THE DREAM

Published by Overachiever Magazine

Human of my dream: barefoot, barefoot,
barefoot.
I was running in my dream, barefoot in the
green,
standing in a field—in a small circle between
the trees.
The flowers tickled my ankles with their
dancing
around the pond. You left footsteps in my sleep,
and I tried to walk the mile you left behind.
We met in a puddle of uncertainty, the pond
between two of us.
I looked at the small waters, my own face was
then watching me.
Yet the face inside the pond belonged to
another girl:
the person before warmth, before knowing
about dreams.
Life finds color and becomes that color—there
is a name for my skin:
Oats, wheats, the honey jarred inside our eyes,
heating us both from within.

I turned my back to the crossroads to face you,
to see you, to feel you.
I sit by the pond, barefoot. Flowers are crowning
my feet, and my gaze coating you.

MOUNTAIN TOP

Up on the height that is blue, tall, triangular,
I feel the hunger to hold you and to devour
    your hunger.
"Let's go higher, there might be eggs."
We go higher, there are no eggs.
"Let's go higher, there might be tea."
We climb to the top, there is no tea.
As we come down, there is a man waiting,
just for you and me.
Eggs, tea, honey to make it sweet.

There are whites, there are blues.
The snow on the top and the blue mountain
    peeking through—
Indigo, lamp black, and a hint of lemon yellow
    too.
An outline runs through it all, but I only feel
    the hues.

BROKEN TOOTH

The jagged chip appears
as my kisses make pink smears
like jam on a scone with rose milk tea.
The whole city blinking somewhere past three
and your hand momentarily stroking my ears.
Then, late afternoons, and the eye dampening
 blue
covering the windows as if the curtains were
 new,
even the ones with a terrible Manhattan view.
The phone rings because I'm still sitting beside
 it,
vibrating where I chide it.
The thin thrum of the telephone in air—
Yet you can't find me. Why? Where?
You ask because you know there is no answer.
The question whirls in circles around us, like a
 dancer.
You stop looking for me when the yellow
 windowbecomes blue.
The city wakes with you.

ICY HEART

It seems I have landed on the island of Asiatic
cheetahs,
as if they would live here—I think they must
die on the ice.
I promised not to sing of death or to cry about
love.
To beg for warmth on a frozen island without
water,
or fruits or people—I'm only trying to hold still
for the last photograph.

The heat of red anger stays under my skin.
Gray days
made the igloos dim where I would hide and
sleep.
I am patient for death, but impatient about the
true heat

from the touch of another being, just their
passing
even on a land without soil, drinkable water, or
monkeys.

TEST OF LOVE

In dreamland, there are promises we make that we keep until the sun glides into the sky. We set a table for the test, to see whose heart aches the most. The one who admires, or the one who is insane?

On the table there is a small round tray. In it are two small cups, half-filled with coffee. One of them contaminated with ricin. I spin the little tray on the little round table. I forgot to mention that the table is covered with an ancient Persian Termeh, that is stained with many drops of heavy coffee. The hot coffee spills but only a drop or two onto the saucer. I'm mixing the poison evenly with the spin, to take one of our heartbeats away quickly. This test is not about pain, but about the carrier of it. There is no winner because this isn't a game.
Both of us are victorious in our courage to risk death for love. But there is a person who is set free at the end of this coffee date. Is it the person who swallows the tainted coffee, or is it the one who lives without their lover?

Once the tray stops and stands still, it's time for one of us to choose their coffee cup. I let you decide because I am grateful toward anything you leave behind for me. In wakefulness, we have eaten together on many occasions. I gave you many bites of fresh food I did not touch and wanted you to finish my coffee. I indented my appetite for the last coffee I will have with you, the one I cannot leave behind.

LULLABY

published by Torrey House Press

Drunk on nectar between the flowers in this
    rooftop garden
without wasting a pinch of bonemeal. I see the
    bulbs open:
pink tutus spinning in each stage of dirt.

But the stem of my favorite flower has a broken
    home.
My soft stem is en pointe, tipping the ground
every time I tiptoe unbalanced. Watching the
    buds awaken—

This city has seeds of flowers like me.
My name is summoned because it sounds like a
    song.
No one told the children flowers evolve into
    fairies,

like caterpillars and butterflies. They just know.
The sky snores in my ear but in tune with a
    sonata.
I dance instead of going to sleep. My hair has
    loosened from a bun,

My bare hands scoop honey from a jar, the
sweet aftermath of a flower.
I pass the window and dance on every rooftop
until I fall into a water rooftop. I become the
grandest tulip.

INTERMISSION

It was in retrospect,
my reappearance alongside myself,
without you. I woke up and thought,
I need to look for you.
In hindsight I knew you weren't there.
I turned to the open fields that were captured in
my bedroom window.
Suddenly I was in Rocky Hill,
an abundance of fall leaves drifting into my
face.
I felt the sharp edges of the maple leaf scar my
cheek,
like the pain of an empty space meant for a
kiss.
In those leaves, I tried to find the pieces of you.
I had forgotten that your being wasn't contingent
on your presence.

SLEEPING ON A SHIP

After I learned about distance, I found my treasure on a boat. It took me long to get used to the nervous stomachache, now seasick and unable to carry my heavy love. .I just wanted to paint, to forget, to get lost in the sharp blue of the sea. Remember what I called it?

"The ocean's color that runs a blade through your eyes."

This was the dream with the reds and the browns. You told me, "I need to protect you" before you went to sleep on the ship that had been still. There was no storm or sign of bad days, but the night is crawling in, running into the daylight like dark watercolor bleeding into white cotton. I had a black coat that I threw on you like a blanket. It was small for you to wear, but perfect to cover you on a cold night on a boat. I always wanted to paint you, undisturbed by the world—uninterrupted by any emotions.

When you are consumed by love, you can no longer see. I became colorblind and lost track of all the red skies or eye-hurting blue seas. Everything was gray, except for blackness of

your hair, your eyes, and your thick eyebrows.
Nothing was white like an empty canvas.
Seasickness shades every page of intense love.

But on that ship where you slept, my canvas was brand new. My palette had red and brown, a bit of pink, and of course, black for the weight of value, sinking the ship we stepped on.

THE MOONLIGHT

In a leap of the moon to when it's full like my
heart,
I waited for you all day, until even the sun left
the sky.

The dust that follows from the sanded land
called desert
is a coat that guards me in a city I cannot walk
barefoot.

The joy of you is a smile I wear with my teeth
and my eyes.
I can smell the dead lilies, the burnt roses, the
spoiled tulips.

The scent of the one you love can be so
intoxicating
like the lulling air of spring and the blur of
gasoline in heat.

I see it all from the distance, there is no water
on the asphalt.
But I see a round sphere of light, and I'm still
waiting for you.

I waited for you all night, even when the
moonlight spilled
into my glass of wine that I drank from the
bottle that is now empty.

LOVE POEM

Do you hear the song of the heat warming us?
It bangs and clicks from the trapped air, but it
still works
 for us.

They've hidden the radiator because the color's
  crusting off,
but I like the copper shapes and the grey scabs
  around it.
The smell of dry cleaners, blow dryers, and
  boxed heaters:
they all remind me of the fever from napping
  under heavy quilts.
Patterns like the radiator, but adored because of
  its pinkish color,
and squares of little homes, housing people and
  cats too tired to move
from the padded couches onto the bed. In a
  parallel universe, or just a dream,
my body is feverish, still, and my eyes are
  warmed with sleep. But you—
You are the one staring at the white paint
  peeling off the ceiling.
Good music is escaping from the street and
  trying to hum with the heat,

the song of the pipes that sing for us in the
winter with its unrhyming beat.
Please, sit down for another round of tea. I'll
read your lines with you.

SUN TALK

I begin to understand the appetizing emotion of
melting butter,
like the way mountain girls want to feel wind in
their hair—
The same sensation I get when I look at you, as
you look at me.
Sunlight still strokes my face whether I try to
look away,
or stare into your eyes. I feel the heat of red
anger from a mistake
I made, and then slowly the warmth of the
honey back in your gaze.
Mountain girls call melting butter wind in their
hair for a reason.
It is post-revolutionary Iran and hijab is
mandatory: A scarf,
long and thick, covers my curly head of hair.
There is wind blowing—
That wind is my friend. It feels my face and
tries to hide in my hair,
until it is released from the mandatory cover,
back into the echo of a mountain.
We are called mountain girls because this is
where we are free.

I let my scarf fall to my shoulders and greet the
    sugar-coated range.
This is where I feel the wind in my hair, and
    taste the honey stirred, sun kiss.

OVERLETTER

Do you mind listening to me again   I ask?
I am the same. Lying down for hours in bed.
Crying in bed, black blotches on the
          pillowcase.
Leaving at noon for a bite of food I do not
          want,
coming home late from a drink I didn't dance
          to
or even feel the heat from—what must I do
                    now?
I wait and I wait, for an answer, popping out of
          you
like the bit of chipped tooth you lost in a fight:
          you
thought you were drunk, but you wanted to
          fight.
Late reply is better than no reply or a
          bad reply.
That is why I still let you look at
          me,
the meaningful, eyebrow risen, eyes widen,
          look
you do. Do you see
                                        this

incredibly meaning
less
gap
that
has
found
itself
between us?
Like
words
just

filling
the page

with
no

Goal!

Just

to

move
on.

But I won't.

FLOWER STORM

Please stay for the next spin of the dial, the
hour
or two following. The next month, the two, the
decade.
The next lifetime and the one that has passed.

They will pour petals and tulip bulbs on our
heads
whether or not we try to run with sugar being
crushed
for us. Don't you see? Everything in this world
is two

Like me and you. But there is only one of us
with a stir
of that sugar cube in dark, dark tea. That is me,
I am the short-lived thunder lighting the night.

When there is a flower storm, rain pours
through tears
And soil becomes gold that falls on my finger.
Don't let this flower be a rose, whose stem will
scar me.

HOLIDAY

The room is bright when the lit candles are
seated
in front of a grand mirror. Red and light pink
fabric
covering almost anything—presents, tables,
myself.
I chose to wear the color that is inside me, I
remember
that I am alive. The yellow of the lights meets
the knit
nicely. Your hand that is cold is warmed by
mine,
and mine by the redness of your smile.
I have a bow and a ribbon to choose for my
hair,
but I will pick whatever is easiest for you to
untie.
Everyday cannot be as light as today, or the few
days,
the short-lived weeks of holiday.
The snow arranges its fall on these days
because it knows,
we will be holding each other: we will be
lighting the candles,

doubling their warmth as we place them in
front of the mirror.

A PIECE

Published by Jaden Magazine

The thin musk layered between lilies and
 dandelions is unreal,
a scent captured between moments of us
 together, interlocking
fingers and strands of hair—I slowly lose the
 fragrant touch
of your caressing hand. Bergamot hints from
 the cold tea,
as we both stand by the window. The street
 presents itself:
A man turns to the cars in front of his store; the
 cars stop
but the drivers wait for the other to come out, to
 de-coat.
An accident—the side mirror of the first car is
 separated.
There must have been a speeding motorcycle
 driver.
Last summer, a similar smell of wet grass and
 patchouli
wavered between me and you. The spoiled
 perfume stained.
You give me a piece of affection—your face
 rests on mine.

You give away the lost senses to a lover you
don't know.
The promise was for me to keep the emotional
charge,
the invisible ink of a hidden poem, an unwritten
love letter
enveloped by my own blood and embedded in
each gaze.
I sent that letter anyway; I wrote to the deaf
man in my dream.

THE PLANE

You were older but my hair still contrasted with
my teeth.
Gray, falling hair and a washed-out colored
suit. Beneath it,
a tired body that was free of fat at last. You had
everything.
But you no longer had that childish look and
wit dripping
from your smile. I was on that plane with you,
seated distant.
We were still hiding, still being a secret even
above land.
I was passing by your seat to request a pillow
for my head,
when I kissed your cheek a bit too long for an
old friend.
I sensed the signal of you telling me to sit
down, lacing
my finger as I left. When I look behind me, I
see facing
me the round eyes of a prince. He has no crown
or rose,
but he is the descendant of a king. And even
though I pose

to be an ordinary among the closest to the
thorned redness,
I know the stem of that flower has a root in my
chest.

PRAYER FOR MY DEAD DOME

I want to tell you to believe in something, just as you would have faith. But believe in something you can never take away; something you know will never get back to you. Just like a dome that will die.

Back home, where you were once a person
more than you are now:
There was a song about you. There was a
prayer for you, an oath
to keep you as human as you always were. But
the promise fell apart.
People forgot, geography expanded beyond the
small lines of a map.
The atlas became your enemy, and I am too far
to call you name—
You were the tailor, the one who sewed my
patterns and prints.

You patched the city of mountains together
with the dead dome,
square and square all by four—turquoise
colored fabric embroidered

with golden thread. It's rough to the touch and
looks wild, but again—
What doesn't? Please take my hand and sew it
to the top of the dome.
I need to feel the spindle as it brings me closer
to the minaret,
As I hear the Azan being sung by an old man I
do not know, but whose voice
I've heard since I was born. The axis of this
shrine aligns with the sun,
But it has a dome that doesn't rise to pray to the
God above. Shame,
Again, and in another lifetime, I will
pray.

THE LAST METER OF THE LINE

Published by the holon project

A faint stroke of a song breaks into my sleep
when I dream: again, a picture of you,
me, and the gap for words I cannot fill.

There is a dent in my tongue for one name.
There is a space of undigested dreams
for the taste of cumin left on my tongue.

I cannot call you. The air has sealed me
with a quiet walk of summer coming
from the still trees that are asleep with us.

There in the hallowed sky, between the hands
of tall, burnt boughs that are interlocked,
I see the gold shimmer of day awakening me.

There in the last meter of the line,
I wait until the last lily is dried
and the wine makes a river between us.

The only way I can travel this meter
Is to become drunk, dance, and dream
and to be the one awakening the trees.

www.ingramcontent.com/pod-product-compliance
Lightning Source LLC
Chambersburg PA
CBHW051750130826
49812CB00033B/1077
9789357213097